PLANTAR FASCIITIS HEALING GUIDE

Exercises and Home Remedies for Heel Pain Instant Cure

By

Erika Robinson

Table of Contents

Introduction

Plantar fasciitis sounds exotic, like the botanical name for a lovely house plant perhaps, but it is not nearly a good thing as the name might suggest. Plantar fasciitis is a foot condition in which the ligaments of the foot arch or plantar fascia gets damaged and so tightens, causing excruciating heel pain. The damage causes this band of tissue to get inflamed or irritated. As you put pressure on it by walking, the pain intensifies.

This condition affects both old and young people. It is more common, however, to see older people experience it. It may be temporary and last for a few days, but the chronic cases can have serious debilitating effects on quality of life. Plantar fasciitis could be a result of

daily wear and tear, the manner of
walking, or lifestyle.

Causes of Plantar Fasciitis

Being able to walk and doing so every day is enough reason to get plantar fasciitis, especially as a result of repetitive stretching and tearing due to too much movement or standing. However, other factors may contribute to it or accelerate its occurrence.

Being overweight. Having a BMI of more than 25 stresses the body. The higher it becomes, the more the stress on your plantar fascia. It stands to reason that grossly overweight people experience plantar fasciitis. Pregnant women often gain a lot of weight, usually in the last stages of pregnancy and by the same token, many experience plantar fasciitis.

Standing for long periods. People that consistently stand for long hours are usually susceptible to developing plantar fasciitis. The more hours you spend on your feet, the greater the pressure put on it and by extension, your plantar fascia. Teachers, nurses, wait staff and factory workers all fall into this category.

Age. The older you get, the longer you have been putting pressure on your feet, literally! Aging may also make your foot arch begin to sag thereby adding more stress on the plantar fascia. It is then no wonder why this condition is common among the elderly.

Foot mechanics. If you are born with flat feet or an excessively arched one, your plantar fascia gets repeatedly overstretched as it tries to compensate for the structural problem.

Accident/Injury. Accidentally landing on a sharp object may lead to the bruising of your plantar fascia. When this happens, the pain will be felt closer to your arch than the heel.

Footwear. Wearing soft soled shoes without proper arch support can result in plantar fasciitis. That your footwear is fashionable does not mean it won't give you pain.

Arthritis. Arthritis sometimes causes an inflammation of the tendons that lie at the base of the feet. This inflammation results in plantar fasciitis. This is a rare occurrence; however, as most people with arthritis never experience this.

Symptoms of Plantar Fasciitis

Sudden pain in your heel may be the first thing to let you know that all is not well. The site of the pain may be the bottom of the heel or at the base of the mid-foot area. While most people complain of sharp pain, some may experience a dull ache that begins as a mild inconvenience.

Sitting or lying down for long may cause the pain to increase the moment you stand up and puts pressure on the affected foot or feet. As you move around and the feet warm up, however, the pain lessens.

How does Plantar Fasciitis get diagnosed?

Not all heel pain is attributable to plantar fasciitis. So make an appointment with your doctor for correct diagnosis. When you make a complaint to your doctor, they will examine your feet, check for tenderness and the exact spot where you feel pain or even take an X-ray of the foot.

The doctor can also help to determine why you are likely to have plantar fasciitis and help you map out a treatment plan or advise on a change in lifestyle. For example, if your plantar fasciitis is brought on by a sudden substantial weight gain, your doctor may advise you to lose weight or draft out a diet plan. Your likelihood of avoiding future episodes may depend on how well you follow your doctor's advice.

How Plantar Fasciitis Progresses?
If left untreated, plantar fasciitis will gradually get worse. You may begin to feel the pain more often and possibly with higher intensity. While an absence of pain means you do not have plantar fasciitis, it begins with a little or sharp pain after some activities or exercise, move to pain before and after exercise,

and evolve to pain at all times, even when at rest.

The pain may also cause you to change the way you walk in a bid to minimize it. This may, in turn, cause you injury in your legs, hips, knees or back.

Long term Effects of Plantar Fasciitis

Leaving plantar fasciitis untreated does not lead to increased pain only; it may result in other unsavory complications. When you continue to participate in high-impact activities without getting the ideal footwear, or you stop the treatment of plantar fasciitis halfway, it gets worse and could result in any of:

Plantar tears: The inflammation and stress of untreated plantar fasciitis can lead to small tears in the plantar fascia. An x-ray or ultrasound can only discover these tears, but you will notice the pain getting worse. Continuing without treatment may increase both the size and number of the tears and eventually result in the rupture of the plantar fascia.

Plantar rupture: Plantar rupture could result from a continued impact on an untreated plantar fascia. Activities such as jogging, hiking or sports put a lot of pressure on the plantar fascia. The rupture causes a loud popping sound alongside agonizing pain, bruising, and the swelling of the foot.

It is better you seek immediate medical help if this occurs. Getting your health back may require you wearing a boot or crutches for a while after a ruptured plantar fascia.

Plantar fibromatosis: Another complication might involve benign nodules growing along the plantar fascia. These slow-growing nodules may at first be undetected, but after some time, the growth rate speeds up and result in walking becoming extremely uncomfortable.

Not all plantar fibromatosis result from plantar fasciitis as some are caused by genetics. However, some researchers hold the belief that an untreated tear in the plantar fascia may lead to plantar fibromatosis.

Heel spurs: When you leave plantar fasciitis untreated, the body tries to protect the arch of your foot and limit damage to it. It does this by sending cells to the point of the problem. These cells then begin depositing calcium there. As the calcium deposits build up, they form sharp knobs that jut out, digging into the fatty pad of the heel. At its most extreme, heel spurs cause agonizing pain with every step taken.

Medical Treatment for Plantar Fasciitis

Plantar fasciitis is first treated with rest, but most times a pain reliever is also prescribed. If it is not resolved within a few weeks, your doctor may outline the available medical treatment options for you. These options range from injections to surgery for severe cases.

Corticosteroid injections: This injection is taken as an outpatient and takes only a few minutes. In order to improve the chances of success, your doctor may use an ultrasound device to determine exactly where to inject. Apart from injecting the corticosteroid to the damaged area, the doctor might choose to apply it directly to the skin of your heel and after that use an electrical current to enable the steroid to pass through the skin.

Physical therapy: Physical therapy cannot be overlooked when treating plantar fasciitis. Your physiotherapist might suggest any of these manual therapy techniques:

- ✓ Joint mobilizations
- ✓ Soft tissue massages
- ✓ Foot Tapping
- ✓ Muscle stretches

These will aid in stabilizing your walk while also reducing the load on your plantar fascia.

Shock wave therapy: This employs sound waves to shock your heel to help you heal. It may, however, come with some side effects such as swelling of the foot, bruises, pain or numbness.

Surgery: This is usually done when all other forms of treatment have been ineffective, and the patient remains in severe pain. The human plantar fascia is somewhat parted from the heel bone to aid the reduction of pressure upon the heel bone. The downside is that it weakens the arch of the foot and may even cause you to lose full function of the foot.

Home Remedies for Plantar Fasciitis

A number of home remedies have proven to be effective in treating plantar fasciitis. These measures are simple and cost-effective.

Rest: Rest allows you to keep weight off your foot and will help the inflammation to go down.

Ice: An ice pack is an effective home treatment for plantar fasciitis. Fill a polythene bag with crushed ice or grab a pack of frozen peas. Wrap a hand towel around it and place on your heel for 20 minutes. Do these 3 or 4 times every day to soothe the pain.

You may also fill an aluminum pan with ice and water then soak your heel in it for 15 minutes. Do these 3 times daily while keeping your toes out of the water.

Pain reliever: Over-the-counter pain-relieving drugs are effectively used in providing pain relief and reducing inflammation.

Shoe inserts: For plantar fasciitis caused by inappropriate footwear, insoles or arch supports will provide the extra cushion and needed support for your feet. Be sure to pick a firm one or get it custom made to increase effectiveness.

Athletic tape: This will give the needed support to your foot. It also creates a kind of restriction that limits moving the foot in a way that will worsen your pain.

Heel cups: These are heel-shaped pads that you put in your shoes to act as cushions, preventing your heel from putting pressure on the plantar fascia as you walk. Heel cups raise your heel so it does not pound the ground with movement. While they may not be as effective as inserts, they cost less.

Night splints: The sleeping state is when we are at our most relaxed. As our muscles relax, we point our feet down. This will make the plantar fascia and Achilles tendon to get shorter. Night splints will keep your feet at an angle of 90 degrees. It means that wearing it while you sleep allows your plantar fascia a good stretch. Night splints are quite effective and can be discontinued once your pain stops.

Walking cast: A walking cast or boot, known as a controlled ankle motion walker, is usually suggested only after other treatments have not worked. The CAM walker makes you rest your foot. The more rest your foot gets, the lesser the pain of plantar fasciitis.

Exercises for Plantar Fasciitis

Exercises are not just important for general well-being; some can help relieve pain for people suffering from plantar fasciitis. Care should be taken to do these exercises in the correct position to prevent making the pain worse. If a stretch hurts, release your hold on that position and relax.

The Calf Stretch: Stand up and face a wall. Taking one step backward, place the flat of your palms on the wall keeping it at shoulder level. If the plantar fasciitis affects one foot only, put that foot back and flex the knee of your other leg, keeping your hips up and tilted towards the wall. Make sure your hands remain straight. You will feel it even as your calf stretches. Count from 1 to 3 then release the hold. Repeat 3 times.

If you have plantar fasciitis in both feet, take the stretch for one foot first and be careful when you flex your knee. Then do the same for the other foot.

The Achilles tendon Stretch: Stand up and face a wall. Taking one step backwards, place the flat of your palms on the wall keeping it at shoulder level. Place the affected foot forward. As you do this, your toes should stay against the wall with your heel on the floor. Flex that knee and push it towards the wall as you feel both the Achilles tendon and plantar fascia stretch. Do this while you keep your other leg straight. Hold position and count from 1 to 5. Repeat 3 times.

The Towel Stretch: As the name implies, you will need a towel for this. Sit straight on a chair, holding a rolled towel at both ends. Now place that towel on the arch of your affected foot and lift your leg off the floor. Extend the leg and keep it horizontal, holding the ends of the towel tightly. Hold the position for 15 to 30 seconds. Change the position of the towel and put it against the back of the ball of your foot. Stretch and hold for 20 seconds.

Repeat the stretch 3 times.

The Toe Stretch: Fall on your knees then place the flat of your palms on the floor, keeping your back straight. Flex your toes. Move your hands backward and bring them towards your knees and feel the stretch. Sit down, supporting your bottom with your heels while you do this. Try to put your hands on your thighs as your toes stretch and the balls of your feet elongate. Hold the position for 10 seconds.

Repeat the stretch 3 times.

The Plantar Fascia Stretch: Get a short step ladder and place the affected foot on the lowest rung keeping the ball of the foot on the edge of the step. Drop your heel downward. This will cause a noticeable stretch in your plantar fascia. Hold the position for 30 seconds. Repeat 3 times.

The Tennis Ball Roll: Sit on the chair and with the tennis ball on the floor, place the affected foot on it. Slowly move the foot up and down. As you do this, the ball massages the sole of your foot. Repeat as often as you wish or until you feel comfortable placing that foot on the floor and walking.

The Roll Out: Sit on a chair and place a cold water-filled plastic bottle on the floor. Place your hurting foot on the water bottle and gently move it up and down. You can do for 5 minutes or till the bottle starts to warm up.

The Arch Strengthening: Sit up straight on a chair and keep your feet flat on the floor. Try to pull your knee up to make a deep arch in your foot without lifting

your toes and heels from the floor. Hold
this position for 3 seconds then relax.
Repeat this 3 times.

The Marble Picker: Sit on a chair and
spread a towel on the bare floor. Put 10
marbles of similar sizes on that towel.
Now place your feet on the towel and use
the affected foot to pick up one marble at
a time then place it by the uninjured
foot. Repeat 10 times.

How massage helps in soothing the pain of plantar fasciitis

Another line of treatment to pursue if you suffer heel pains is massage. Massage is not just a natural method of pain relief; it also comes without the negative side effects often associated with many of the pain-relieving medications.

Combining massage with stretching exercises is one of the best routes you can take in treating plantar fasciitis.

Method: Sit in a comfortable position. Place the affected foot on the knee of your other leg. Now put your thumbs in the middle of the sole of your foot and massage gently. Move your thumbs up, down and to the sides of your sole while you keep massaging. Continue for 5 minutes.

Yoga and Plantar Fasciitis

The number one advice usually given to people with plantar fasciitis is to rest.

And by rest, a lot would automatically give up every form of physical activity and laze on the couch until the pain resolves.

But if yoga is an integral part of your lifestyle, it is not only difficult to give up, but it may also be counter-intuitive. Since stretching of the calves is one of the effective ways of treating plantar fasciitis, many of the yoga stretches actually help with plantar fasciitis. Care should be taken however, not to worsen the condition by improper alignment.

What not to do when doing yoga with plantar fasciitis
You may injure the tissues at the sole of your foot and make your plantar fasciitis worse if you consistently place your foot and ankle outside of the neutral position. A neutral foot is one in which the heel bone is vertical. The heel bone should neither tip inward or outward. Having the heel bone in a vertical position allows

for healthy weight-bearing in the inner and outer balls of the feet, and also in the inner and outer heels.

Ankles that slope toward each other thereby bringing the inner arches toward the floor (pronation) and those that slant away from each other and deepen the inner arches (supination) are both outside the neutral position. Either of these can aggravate the plantar fascia.

In effect, overpronating or over supinating your feet while practicing yoga with plantar fasciitis will continue the damaging pattern that led to or contributed to the condition. Your feet may feel worse after yoga practice, and you may even conclude that yoga, and not how you position your foot, is the problem.

How to properly align your feet and knees

Follow these tips to refine the positioning of your feet and knees using common yoga poses.

The Mountain: "Stand straight with your feet apart and your middle toes pointed upward." If your ankles slope toward each other with your inner arches dropping toward the mat (pronation), the effect is that you are standing on the inside of your heels.

If your ankles are parted slightly away from each other, and you have your inner arches lifted and also have the bases of your big toes lifting up off the mat, known as the supination, then you are standing on the outside of your heels. You may need to have someone sit behind you looking at your heels to look out for these mistakes.

Correct your position by lifting each heel and placing it such that you are standing on the center of each heel. Press down with every corner of each foot so that your weight is distributed among them all. Hold this position for several seconds and learn the sensations that are associated with this neutral foot and ankle alignment.

The Chair Pose: As you relax your body from the mountain pose, place your hands on your hips. Inhale while bending your knees and take note if your knees tend to point inward toward your big toes or outward toward your little toes. Aim your knees toward the center of your feet by tracking them between your second and third toes. Press your feet down and straighten your knees as you let air out of your nose while keeping your knees in position. Repeat several times.

By working toward neutral feet and knees during your yoga practice and your everyday life, you may begin to see the symptoms of plantar fasciitis disappear.

Effects of Food on Plantar Fasciitis

'Let food be your medicine and medicine your food' is so bandied about that we might start to view it as a phrase without any measure of truth. But in this case, Hippocrates was right! What you put in your mouth can either soothe the pain of plantar fasciitis by reducing inflammation of the plantar fascia, or it can aggravate inflammation leading to an increase in pain level.

Foods that aggravate the pain of plantar fasciitis

These foods are known as inflammatories. They should be cut out of your diet or reduced to the barest minimum in order to see a positive change. Processed sugars, saturated fats, trans fats, and salt are all inflammatories.

White bread. White bread is made from flour with most of its fiber removed.

Fiber encourages a feeling of fullness and improves blood sugar control. White bread, stripped of fiber, increases the level of inflammation in the body.

Soda. The sugar contained in soda leads to an increase in the level of uric acid in the body. Uric acid, in turn, drives inflammation and insulin resistance.

Hamburgers. Processed meats are higher in advanced glycation end products (AGEs) than other meats. They include hotdogs, salami, sausages, prosciutto, and ham. AGEs are a leading cause of inflammation.

Margarine. Margarine is a common source of trans fats. These artificial trans fats are formed by adding hydrogen to unsaturated fats and help in extending the shelf life of processed foods but cause inflammation in the body.

Alcoholic drinks. While a drink or two may be fine, a high intake of alcohol may increase inflammation in the body.

Other inflammatories to avoid are candy, snack bars, mayonnaise, potato chips, fish sticks, fried chicken, pizza, aspartame, hot dogs, etc.

Anti-inflammatories and their effects on plantar fasciitis

Minerals and compounds such as calcium, magnesium, Vitamin C, and methylsulfonylmethane (MSM), have a beneficial effect on plantar fasciitis by reducing inflammation and by extension, pain. Anti-inflammatories are usually fruits and vegetables as well as some high-quality animal products.

Spinach. This vegetable is one of the most effective anti-inflammatories ever. It contains magnesium, calcium, Vitamin C, and MSM.

Orange. The citrus fruit is chock full of Vitamin C, calcium, and MSM; all of which help in reducing inflammation.

Tuna and Salmon. Wild-caught tuna and salmon are chockfull of Omega 3 fatty acid. Omega 3 is an essential compound for reducing inflammation. Pumpkin and flax seeds are also great sources.

Tomatoes. Tomatoes are high in lycopene; an antioxidant and anti-inflammatory, as well as Vitamin C and potassium. To maximize the benefits of tomatoes, cook in a little olive oil.

Cherries. It does not really matter whether your preference is for the sweet or tart variety. Both have anti-inflammatory properties and will help with plantar fasciitis.

Broccoli. This cruciferous vegetable is rich in sulforaphane. Sulforaphane is an antioxidant and does not allow the human body to give in to inflammation when taken in the right quantities. An easy way to reap the benefits of broccoli is to make it one of your five-a-day vegetables.

Berries. Anyone of strawberries, blueberries, loganberries or bilberries can be eaten as part of an anti-inflammatory diet. Their power resides in the antioxidants they all contain called anthocyanins. Although berries are classified as fruit, they contain a very low amount of sugar.

Green tea. The last thing you may want to do when feeling the pain of plantar fasciitis is to make tea, but it may truly bring you much-needed relief. Green tea components are a surprisingly high content of epigallocatechin-3-gallate or EGCG. This antioxidant called EGCG also works as an anti-inflammatory substance that helps reduce pains from plantar fasciitis. EGCG reduces the production of cytokine, a pro-inflammatory, in the body.

Turmeric. This bright yellow spice with its smoky flavor is a powerful anti-inflammatory. Brewed as a tea, added to smoothies, or your favorite slow-cooked soup, the curcumin in turmeric will do you a world of good.

Traveling with Plantar Fasciitis

For plantar fasciitis that does not resolve within a few weeks, it becomes impossible to put your life on hold and wait for complete healing. It means you may need to go on a business trip, a vacation, a family wedding, an out-of-state job interview, or any of the myriad reasons why humans travel from one place to another. While you may not be able to prevent traveling, you can make sure you stay as comfortable as is possible when traveling with plantar fasciitis.

And for parents, it should be a relief to know that you can still plan that theme or national park outing without allowing plantar fasciitis to put a crimp in your style.

Pack good shoes: It may be a letdown not to be able to wear your favorite strappy sandals to that cousin's wedding, but your health should come first. Wear supportive shoes like a Birkenstock when you travel and groove on anyway. As a backup, do not forget to take with you good quality arch support inserts.

Stretching: More than ever, when you travel is when you should need to make sure that your stretching game is on point. Stretch several times every day without waiting for the pain to remind you to perform the routine.

Ice therapy: Take along with you a reusable water bottle and fill it with ice either from fast food stops (if taking a road trip) or your hotel's ice machine. Once you get to your destination or are taking a rest, roll it under your foot for 20 minutes.

Pain relievers: Even if you have been strictly following a natural method of treatment without any form of medication, it is advisable to take along an over-the-counter medication like ibuprofen when traveling. If the pain ever gets too much, it may be what will save you from being able to participate fully in activities or sitting on the sidelines.

Conclusion

If you walk a lot, participate in sporting activities, hold some particular jobs or grow old, chances are you will experience plantar fasciitis at one time or another in your lifetime. The important thing is to follow a treatment plan that suits you, make possible lifestyle changes, and try to avoid the triggers. Although plantar fasciitis can be painful and could hinder you from performing day-to-day activities, the condition is not in particular life-threatening. It is treatable with necessarily going for a medical option although it is important to get diagnosed by and discuss a treatment plan with qualified medical personnel.

Get to know your body, improve your posture and manner of walking, avoid inflammatory foods, and plantar fasciitis will become a thing of the past.

Books by the Same Author

1. <u>Cognitive Behavioral Therapy Techniques: How to Manage Anxiety and Depression Using CBT – Control Your Thinking, Emotions, and Behavior</u>

2. <u>Intermittent Fasting for Women: How to Lose Weight Without Exercise, Boost Energy, Reverse Diabetes, And Prevent Cancer – Slow Down the Aging Process</u>

3. <u>Ketogenic Diet for Beginners: Simple Keto Recipes and Diet Plan to Lose Fat, Heal Your Body, and Boost Energy</u>

4. <u>Adrenal Fatigue Solution: Powerful Methods to Boost Your Energy, Improve Metabolism, And Stimulate Your Hormones</u>

5. <u>How to Reverse Fibromyalgia Cookbook: Recipes and Meal Plan to Relieve Symptoms and Treat Root Cause</u>

6. <u>How to Reverse Hashimoto's Thyroiditis: Eliminate Root Cause and Heal Hypothyroidism Symptoms Naturally</u>